the stars within us

high frequency spiritual poetry

oana stefanescu

Soft Altitude Publishing
www.softaltitudepublishing.com

the stars within us – high frequency spiritual poetry
by Oana Stefanescu

Published by Soft Altitude Publishing
Ottawa, ON, Canada
www.softaltitudepublishing.com

Copyright © 2022 Oana Stefanescu

All rights reserved. No portion of this book may be reproduced in any form without permission from the publisher.

Cover and artwork by Oana Stefanescu

Author photo by Alex Stefanescu

ISBN 978-1-7387127-0-0

Printed in Canada

First Edition

I would like to dedicate *the stars within us*, with all of my heart and all of my love, to every single member of my family, all past, present, and future.

I would never be who I am, and who I am becoming, without you – thank you.

In love and immense gratitude,

Oana

before you begin

the stars within us - high frequency spiritual poetry is a collection of poems which are meant to take you, the reader, on a journey of spiritual self-discovery. They touch on various subjects intended to spark a remembering within your soul of who you really are, and the happiness with which you are meant to live your life.

As you walk together with the narrator through different settings, stories, and exercises, you will get to peek behind the veil, into the vast and mysterious world of spirit and universal energy.

This entire collection was channeled. As I sat down to write, I heard each poem in my mind almost in its entirety. The words may at first seem simple, but the concepts are something to contemplate and to meditate upon slowly.

While I have been writing poems for years, I never felt as strong a calling to create an entire collection, and to share it with you, as I did now.

the stars within us is meant to inspire you and support you on your spiritual journey of growth and self-discovery, and to empower you to energetically create the most positive and magical life you possibly can for yourself.

I wish this for you with all of my heart, and I hope that my words bring you the most positive energetic shifts.

Stay present within your being, and notice any changes you feel after reading these poems. It might take a single moment, or maybe weeks, but your energy will shift.

May your journey be filled with love and abundance,

Oana

P.S.

Please remember, you are everything
that you have always been waiting for,
because you have

- we all have -

the stars within us.

the stars within us

high frequency spiritual poetry

the poems within

good morning	14
the veil	16
helping hands	18
the voices inside	20
the civilizations within	22
the rust	24
a lot to say	26
ancestors	28
ancestral healing	30
stars in our eyes	32
this time	34
against the odds	36
karma	39
our mission	41
awareness	43
soft focus	45
what does it mean to see?	47
inner peace	49
alignment	51
close your eyes	53

psychic	55
clouds	57
the fear of falling	59
when your world implodes	61
when your heart breaks	65
broken	69
your smiling soul	71
see through your heart	73
creating from the heart	77
other people	79
true love	81
multidimensional	83
other beings	85
healing	87
breathe	89
meditate	92
return to earth	94
new earth	96
fall asleep	98
fall in love	100

imagine	102
create	104
high frequencies	106
gratitude	108
allow	110
opportunities	112
purpose	114
impact	118
discover	120
the stars within us	122

good morning

since you're here,
will you take a walk with me,
through the lightness of the light?
we have walked together before
I remember it well,
it was both a short and long time ago
partly in the light of the day,
and partly in the light of the night.

is it time to remember,
even if only a tiny fragment
of who you really are?

what you know of yourself,
and the story you have lived
is only a split-second memory
of what really is.

you are such a divine
and beautiful being

with so much to offer to us all,
I wish you begin remembering
before the leaves begin to fall.

you are,
yes, you are,
and your guides
can see it from afar.

you are the "I am"
and you will always be
a divinely beautiful being
immortal, and free
powerful, and as glorious
as can be.

good morning,
welcome,
and thank you
for taking this walk with me.

the veil

if we take a look around
we will see what we can see
with our eyes in the 3d.

it seems so real
but you see,
what is so solid
is just a shimmer,
compared to what's free.

what if our real eyes
are actually closed?
then what is it that we see?

it is all a mist
of living and things
feeling all too palm and fist
a splinter from our collective memory.

oana stefanescu

there are various degrees
to the density of this mist
this veil of fog over our eyes
as if painted in a frieze.

wait, was it always there?

the more the mist lifts
the more it is clear
that we must go on
feeling what we really feel.

only then will our real eyes
begin to open,
to the magnificence of
what is, what was, and
what will be.

Are you ready to begin
lifting the veil?

helping hands

you can hold my hand,
or just know that it is there
please take what you need
and what comforts your heart.
this heart of mine is big enough
to hold you too.

whether I use my hands or not
my thoughts are with you.

please remember
love is everywhere,
and it is free
there is so much
love around us
that our perception
cannot see.

there are helping hands
to hold us

and to guide us on our way
from around
and from above
from sight
and from the mind.

each has a different touch
a different feel

they all love us deeply
and encourage us
to do the same
for ourselves
for each other
for mother earth,

and we too become
helping hands
as, and after,
we find our way.

the voices inside

out of all of the voices inside,
that hide inside your mind
which ones are real?
which ones should you
follow to the depths
so that you can finally heal?

are all of them you,
or are they something else?
you need to figure this out, first,
it's up to you and no one else.

you might have gotten so used to them
that they sound like familiar friends,
but only a couple speak truth
while the others rattle and sway,

sending you this way and that,
while you waste away
your precious moments every day.

survey your voices inside,
and try to find,
the one that really speaks,
you.

that's the right frequency

from the many you carry inside
the one that never had
anything to hide,
and is ready to be
your guide.

the civilizations within

we sometimes wonder
about those who walked
the earth before us,
and we ponder where
they've gone.

what happened to them?
how did they live?
what were their stories?
where can we find them,
or read them,
so that we know
better,
what to avoid?

were they really
more advanced?
was their magic real?
if so,
how come they've gone?

what about their legacy?
what about their memory?
do only their names
remain?

we know
them
and we feel
them
from a distant memory
because they've not really gone.

we carry them
encoded
and encrusted,
those civilizations,
deep within
us.

the rust

step one is
make a choice
through the rubble and the noise
as the Legos clatter to the ground
drowning thoughts in their sound,
with one hand sticky from purée,
decide when,
today's the day.

step into awareness
anxious readiness,
fear of the unknown
and excitement for mysteries
so ready to be shown.

then sift, sift, sift,
and sift some more
until you find the precious metals
from before.

the silver

and the gold,

the moldavites

and the dust,

separate it all

from the "you"

they turned to

rust.

a lot to say

your voice has a lot to say
just give it the light of day
a bit of your ear
and a bit of your heart
some of your energy
and then it can start
to give you advice
and to give you direction
and the knowledge to help you
direct your intention.

let it flow,
and do not judge
that flurry of juice and sludge
that you've been holding
back so tight
kept so deeply
compressed and
out of sight.

once the flood begins

let it clear

your path,

your voice,

your love,

your wrath,

so that it may finally speak

and you may finally hear

that magical diamond voice,

because it has

a whole lot

to say

to you.

ancestors

they came before us
so that we could be
children of the earth
beautiful and free

they lived their lives
the best they could
and laid the groundwork
as well as they would

our line has come to turn
and our turn has come in line

to finish up their groundwork
and sow the seeds they couldn't find

it is now our time
to plant those seeds
to work with our psyche
and find our needs

and understand
what was really left
upon this land

it's not just about earth
or about seeds
but rather more
about the energies

which are not linear
and which do not end
ready to move you
bend after bend

our ancestors
laid down the path
for us to come
to save them
to save our future
and to save ourselves.

ancestral healing

we are a circle

we are where it ends

and where it begins

and we can do

the most incredible things.

since we are all one

and the one is all

when one heals

we heal both big and small.

when we came

into this world

our circle was filled

with dreams and wishes

that were never built.

the grief and the pain

and maybe visions insane

have followed us from the past,
to be resolved at last
and give us clear way
to live a happier day,

while also healing
deep wounds
for those beloved figures,
as our past lingers.

ancestral healing
is a blessing to fulfill
as you take
your time to do it
your heart grows -

bigger,
bigger,
and brighter still.

stars in our eyes

the truth will never die
because someone will always know
what some try so hard
to bury in words and snow

we have stars in our eyes
that we cannot see
yet when we look to the skies
we can finally be

open to our true potential
and see what we must see
a world becoming less hidden
a world ready to be free.

oana stefanescu

this time

visions and feelings from
within and outside ourselves
carry a weight and depth
that can shift this century.

we can make what we envision
there is nothing we can't create
our inner power is glorious
and we are here to ascend.

ascension is a shift
it is an evolution
a growing of our souls
the widening of our eyes
the living through our hearts
and the expansion of our minds.

we were meant for so much more
all of us were
all of us knew it
and all of us now know for sure,

even if we cannot explain
the feeling or the thought

we are here to return
the earth and ourselves
to the beauty and the glory
that we were made of.

all starting with a thought,
we are ready

this time.

against the odds

against the odds
we're going to win
we'll take your car
and go for a spin

down the highways
of light
and light-ways of change
we'll take a look
at a whole new range
a whole new arrangement
than you would have chosen

under your command
the whole world
would have
frozen

under your gaze
and beneath your boot,

oana stefanescu

it wasn't our place
below your foot.

against the odds
we've risen right
when even the clock
was stuck to night.

our hearts spoke the truth
they knew what was right

and we followed them through
to the end of the fight.

we did what we could
to stay on our track

even with those shadows
embedded in our back.

the stars within us

our world was always ours
our souls always knew
and deep in your heart,
you knew it too.

we couldn't have done it
we wouldn't have
beaten the odds,

if it wasn't

for you.

oana stefanescu

karma

the energies that follow us
come back round
and round
to nudge us to balance
the light and the sound.

lifetimes away
yet here once again
to ask us to repay
all we did and say
in a life from yesterday.

we can clear it up
if we work hard
live well and kind
and stay on our guard,
maybe this life is the last
for clearing our card.

wouldn't that be something,

to be rid of the weeds

that have taken root

in our souls

from past misdeeds?

our mission

maybe we were sent here
on a mission to be free
maybe we wanted to be here
so that we can see

the marvels and the miracles
the moves and the divine
power that is within us,
when we won't be stopped
this time

let us find joy and happiness
in the simple, and in the everyday
like the comfort of touch
and the experience of taste

we must take it all in,
and enjoy all that we won't have
in dimensions less dense,
when we'll be
outside ourselves.

awareness

to know who we are
and what we're here to do
to know how we feel
and then to share it too

not just with others
but with fragments of ourselves
who are watching
and waiting
and guiding...

let's do what we love
and see what makes us laugh
let's do everything with heart
because then we can be sure
we are right where we should be
and we won't wander anymore.

we know what we're here to do
we know it in our souls.

it's time to let the clutter fall
and not allow distractions anymore

it's time to bring awareness
and centre it at our core.

soft focus

sometimes soft focus will let you see
something or other, that is said, cannot be

once you relax your body
and soften your gaze
you may begin perceiving a light or a haze
even shapes of energy right in your space

there is so much more around us
that we have learned not to see
so of course, seeing gets dismissed
as quick as can be.

yet you have the power,
and you can do it right away
do your best to relax
allow your breath to sway

then as you look around your space,
take it slowly and in pace

with a soft gaze, and a clear mind
look for variations in the air,
and what will you find?

you might see different textures,
colours, or forms made of light

if you feel that you saw something,

you are probably right.

what does it mean to see?

if you think you saw something,
you probably did.

there is more to this world
than we have been taught,
and spirit is just about
planting you,
that seed.

in fact, it may well be that
there are more worlds than one,
just as some believe that
there really are none.

can you imagine
multiple layers
of existence,
each with their own thoughts
and their own minds
living by us, but not really here?

when you see

it means you looked

and that's more than most people do

if you saw, now you know

that you also have access

to the door

that will lead you to

so

much

more.

inner peace

keeping inner peace
gets harder
or easier
depending on how you play.

it's all about guiding your thoughts
down the roads of your choosing
walking, biking, rolling down
sometimes even without a sound.

but as soon as you no longer choose
which avenue to peruse,
when you take a break and let others drive,
they would choose differently
than you would inside.

inner peace is a garden,
a courtyard, so vulnerable
to the whims of change
and to the winds of life.

oana stefanescu

tend to it softly,
carefully, every day
you must
check on the flowers,
the soil, and the ground,

how is the sunshine?

how are the sounds?

inner peace is worth more than gold,
more than any property ever sold,

because that garden is
the very foundation
on which to grow
both young
and old.

alignment

to be in alignment you must
stack things just right
build with them a pyramid inside,
with a great big base
to ground you in your space.

you need your inner peace,
so that you can be and breathe
exactly who you are.

listen only to the guidance
that speaks to your heart.

clean out the cobwebs
from your eyes and from your ears
because it may really have been years
since you have seen and heard
what rings of truth…

own that power,

your fuel of stardust inside,

you are so much more than a human

on this bumpy earthen ride.

build your pyramid

and take good care

to charge it by the moon

if you so dare.

close your eyes

close your eyes
like you would meditate,
but stay in that darkness in full awareness.

breathe deeply and gently,
and allow yourself to see…

you can connect in this space,
without time, without place,
to wisdom and knowledge
from here and from afar
as long as you're aware
of what you truly are.

allow the images, sounds, and light,
to come into your awareness with delight.

this is the space of spiritual connection
and you are welcome to visit it
any time you like.

it's the very same space of mind
where sages and masters have also been,

and you can visit too,
because they are really you.

you can ask questions,
or just take in what comes.

so, close your eyes and take a look
you can do it, I promise you,

have no fear, have no worry
there are no mistakes
when you work from your heart;

and do tell us what you see
when you
close your eyes.

psychic

we are all psychic
we all have the gift
for some it's been easier to access
while some just resist.

letting go of fear
and allowing the tips to come
helps you see new signs
one by one.

it is being more open
to that which is less seen
feeling what is less felt
hearing the unheard
and knowing what has not yet been.

we all have these moments,
but we do not recognize the change
instead of being grateful,
we worry about being strange.

yet soon enough you'll notice
that you can see and hear more
you somehow start to know things
that you've never known before.

when this happens, feel the joy
your life will be so much more

as you accept your gifts,
and begin to use them
in love,
your heart will soar.

clouds

have you noticed
have you seen
how beautiful the sky has been
how lovely and how bright?

there is something different
about the light
about the colours
of day and night

I watch the sky
everyday in awe
everyday more delighted
with what nature can draw

a moving, living painting
of shadows and of light
every moment, brilliant
and everything is right

as it should be

and as it is

living under such a sky

filled with wonders floating by.

the fear of falling

sometimes the ground,
the under, the platform
on which you stand
is suddenly much thinner
than it should be.

sometimes the ground,
that's supposed to hold you up
appears ready
to let you go

where would you fall,
if the "under you" shall go?
can you fall any further
than where the ground, itself, is?

what feels like a catastrophe,
a catastrophic loss of balance,
is as much an illusion as anything else
make sure to look before you fall.

perhaps the fear of falling

is much worse than the fall itself

and then, if it happens,

you will just

get

more....

grounded.

and your fear of falling,

at least this number in line,

will also fall

back into the essence

of what holds you steady.

when your world implodes

that day you get that call,
that message,
or you see that piece of news
that shakes up your intellect
and the very socks on your feet -

at that moment, your world
your thoughts, your mind,
your understanding
feel just like your socks do,
and start peeling themselves off,
away from your core,
as your world,
as you know it,
implodes.

how do you now make
heads or tails, or even torsos
of this ouroboros of
mind boggling decisions,

so easy to make,
and so very destructive
to the very world
that they're made in.

a deep breath in,
exhale slowly as your body
turns to gray from this knowing,

as you shake in anger
and in disbelief
at what humans are capable of
doing to their own kind.

that knowing will never leave
you, or your perspective
because the filter has been removed.

the stars within us

your will is stronger now
than ever before,
to set things right
in your mind
and in your soul.

are you ready to
take action
in the physical world?

oana stefanescu

when your heart breaks

let me just come out and say it straight
this life comes with a whole lot of pain
all kinds of it, at varying degrees
and it always leaves a mark.

did we sign up for it,
as we signed our soul contracts?
everything probably looked
so easy to us then,
as ethereal beings
so full of love and light,
with the universe at our fingertips
as we watched the unfolding
from the other side of the veil.

when your heart breaks, it comes
with an amnesia of certain functions
suddenly, fog overtakes the mind,
as the pain spreads
throughout the torso,

oana stefanescu

and seeps into everything
that's nearby.

you have to feel it, sit in it, like a chair,
like a rotten one with broken planks,
with rusty nails left in there,
broken, unsteady, cold,
and slippery from moss and fungus
it probably doesn't even stand right,
so steady it on a rock,
on the side with the shorter leg.

you're lucky, look,
it still has 4 legs,
even while having been
abandoned and forgotten
in the woods.

how did it even get there?

see? feel it and then move on.
come up with an analogy or a story,
to describe what it is
that's taking up your space inside.

it's yours,
your space,

take good care of it.

remember that your heart cannot break,
unlike that hypothetical chair
left in the woods.

your pain is real,
and that feeling
is the energy you need to process,

by allowing it to run its course
until it's gone.

then, take that energy

and transform it

into transcendently beautiful love,

by doing something

that brings a smile

to your very soul.

broken

we are all broken,
none of us are whole
we used to remember
but we don't,
anymore.

we had to break
in order to come
into our lifetime
on earth as we are
forgetting that
we're all part of
the light of a star.

we are all broken
when we are apart
yet together
we are whole
a family
an entity

filled with love

and with so much more.

we are all broken

we have been split

into bits

and to heal

we must reintegrate

that which we miss

that we don't even know

but that

is what

this lifetime

is for.

your smiling soul

your soul is a being that encompasses
so much more
than who and what you are.

it is the very window
through which you live your life
and through which you get to see
as much as your vision can hold.

you choose how narrow or wide
your window is, looking
onto the vision of your life.

the sunshine warming your face
and the breeze swaying your curtains
so that they may caress
and embrace you
as you allow the sunshine
straight into your heart.

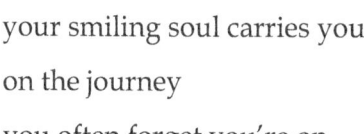

your smiling soul carries you
on the journey
you often forget you're on

watching your every move
so proud of your every decision
no matter what it may be
because you are doing
and you are being
exactly
what you are meant to be.

see through your heart

I heard something the other day
that I found absolutely beautiful:
"see through your heart"
said this wonderful astrologer.

this brings a new perspective,
a new view in all regards,
because, if we start
seeing through the heart
our lens changes dramatically,
don't you think?

once you start
seeing through your heart,
your life will change.
think about it,
actually no,
feel into it.
imagine leading
your life through feeling,

through your intuition,
leaving behind all the things
that you were told,
and finally beginning
to do what feels right,
what makes your heart happy.

imagine living in a way
that makes your heart feel as warm
and as bright as the sun we know.

the happier you are,
the brighter you shine
out onto the world.

when you see through your heart,
you remove yourself
from the seat of judgement
that never made any
positive difference,

the stars within us

and only ever brought
negativity which
dipped your energy
down
below
your
grounding.

imagine your life lived
from a place of love and creativity,
as you slide deeper into
an understanding
of you,
of them,
of it all,

and you get to touch
the hand of your dream

to which you are

getting closer with every breath

as you see it

all

though

your

heart.

creating from the heart

what would you create
when you start seeing through
and following through
with what feels best
in your beautiful heart?

what magic would pour out
of your mind,
of your fingertips,
and into your life
when you follow the path
which makes your soul
smile like the brightest star?

how would that magic
in turn make you feel?
and what would it do
for the world around you?
would anything stay the same?

of course not.
this time there will be
much
more
light.

creating from the heart,
will make the sun shine even
from within the hearts of raindrops;

see them splatter light everywhere,
as they follow their own course
through time and space,
and they wash the earth anew.

welcome
to a brand-new earth,
an old earth
made new by you.

other people

we are all magical beings,
come here to stay and play,

sometimes we do it right,
and sometimes we lose our way.

we choose our dreams and try so hard
to get close to them one day.

we come here with the best intentions,
then life catches us like clay.

when we lose track of who we are,
what does our soul say?

sometimes our soul speaks through
the people around us everyday,

they are our mirrors, here to show us
what we're missing from before.

other people are our teachers and guides
who can open up the cosmic door

where we can reclaim lost parts of us,
so that we may soar
up high enough

to reach

the stars

within us,

that might sometimes seem too far

for us

to reach

alone.

true love

when you meet your true love,
time can stand still,
like a scene from a movie
that we all have seen.

true love is that magic
that makes lifetimes align,
because you probably have
met before, in time.

the universe brings you together,
because you were meant to be,
together like fated rhymes
in the most beautiful poetry.

true love is a gift
and what everything is made of
what the universe has given
so we may concentrate and create
exponentially higher waves

around us and within,
bringing healing and alignment
through where its frequencies reach in.

true love is when your heart is round
with warmth and full of light
when everything in life has meaning,
and every wrong transmutes to right.

in love, as if with magic
all of life rushes towards the goal
and finally, and with great expectations,
everything becomes whole.

multidimensional

we are multidimensional beings
we exist on many planes
we are made of energy
and can ride in many lanes

all at once.

the energy we embody
is only a fraction of our souls
so this life that we are living
is just one of many roles.

oana stefanescu

other beings

there is no way that we are alone
in this vast universe
that is our home.
we are beings made of energy,
so is everything that we see
and so is everything
that we imagine cannot really be.

sometimes when our planes align,
we come to catch a glimpse,
and it reassures us that we are part
of the wheel of life that extends
beyond the textbooks written
to keep us locked
in small understandings,
and limited consciousness.

because once we see,
and once we expand,
our world will transform,

completely, for the better
in ways yet unknown.

other beings are just like us,
but most know more,
with hearts and minds expanded
beyond our capacity to even imagine.

we will join them one day
in their level of understanding
of the real laws of the universe
and we will thrive.

then will come our turn
to care for beings ready to learn
and to help them grow,
as we did,
a very long time ago.

healing

bring the focus
back to you
and everything you need,

find the shadows
you've been hiding
they need to be freed.

shadows may seem dark
but under light
they fade,

as do the stories
that they carry
so heavily weighed

with sorrows and pains
bringing on
traumas and triggers

when you least expect
the darkness throws at you
some facts and figures.

healing is becoming witness
to the parts of you
in need of light,

and taking care
with love and patience
of the parts you want to fight.

healing is acceptance
of you and as you are
making clear your desire.

find your purpose
and awaken your dream,
the one that guides you from within.

breathe

as you breathe in
the oxygen that brings life into you,
inhale it in as light,
a bright, beautiful light
that cleanses, heals, and transforms
your body, your mind, and your soul.

as you exhale,
exhale the light into the world,
and brighten up
the stems, the petals, the seeds
in everything
and everyone
in your outer world.

feel your body
with every breath,
and allow your tension to dissolve,
letting more go,
with each exhale…

oana stefanescu

breathing in the light,
and purging out the dust
that has for years settled
in the nooks and craters
of your being.

with each breath,
your mind gets quieter,
your body softer,
and your grounding stronger.

deeply feel,
how much you were meant to be
here and now,
in the expression that is you,
in this expression that is your life

now.

breathe.

meditate

to meditate is to quiet your mind
and begin to notice every kind
of thought that sweeps across
like the wind of a win or of a loss,
in the vastness of the space
that's always rolling in a race.

to meditate is to step back,
to allow, and to give slack
to whatever comes up for you
see it, then feel it too
just gaze from a distance
as you sit comfortably in the instance.

keep breathing and just see
all that comes and wants to be,
your thoughts are not you,

they will change if you will them to,
but to meditate is to separate,
to see the difference while you wait.

to meditate is to find your calm,
to soothe your soul with quiet balm
anytime you need to find your grounding
to fix your footing or your standing,

meditate from wherever you are,
slow down and find your inner star.

return to earth

time passed us by
and the wind blew strong
slowly our senses grew numb
to the earth and her song.

we must return to the earth
we must hear her voice again
we must grow back our ears
that the machinery has slain.

industry surely has its place
but the earth gives us life
what needs our protection more?
certainly not our incessant strife.

it is time to look once more
to nature and learn again to hear
the wisdom of the ages
in whispers sharp and clear.

oana stefanescu

the animals and the plants
have so much to teach,
and to re-learn our way
we must hear their speech.

who we are
and where we've been
is all recorded in the earth
soon coming to be seen

along with knowledge
about what our life can be
once we understand the workings
of true nature and our history.

new earth

it's time to make our way
back to where we've been
energetically
vibrationally
in lives we've never seen

but soon we will
as the frequencies elevate
our bodies,
closer to our souls

some of us will see it
some will be right behind us
and others will be there soon

we will all make it there
at different rates
of understanding
of consciousness expanding
and of permeating light.

new earth

is old earth

but evolved to a state

of her truer nature

in a higher frequency rate.

life will become freer

more fulfilling

and more beautiful

for all of us

as we move closer into

the patterns and the way

in which we

were all meant to live.

we will get to see it

feel it and live it

soon and together

in new earth.

fall asleep

if you have trouble sleeping,
remember your breathing,
your friend, your ally, your guide,
as you muster your courage
to go along for the ride

into the space of the collective unconscious
into the space that really reminds us
of the rocks we must kick out of our own way
to get the messages in the night,
so we can save our day.

stretch out and find your comfort,
use as many pillows as you need
and allow a few thoughts of gratitude
to sneak in before you clear your mind
and find your quiet within.

with every inhale,
fill your body with light,

your heart with love,
then exhale,
and feel yourself growing heavier,
sinking into a comfortable darkness,

sinking deep and deeper into your bed
that holds you in a warm
and firm embrace.

all that matters now,
is your slow, deep breathing,

the powering off
of any disturbance of the mind,
the complete softening of the body,
and the trust that all is,
absolutely,
and exactly,

as it should be.

fall in love

I might've mentioned it before,
but, dear friend, I'll say it again,
because words can be beautiful and magical
and because they matter so;

you are here to love,
to experience this world,
and to find your own way.

allow yourself to enjoy
all of the things
that you crave,
and better yet,
allow yourself to enjoy your days
as they come,
and notice what is beautiful,
magical,
or hilarious,
in the mundane.

the mundane is after all,
not the mundane at all.
it is actually a reef of experiences
just waiting to be snorkelled by.

don't write anything off,
instead, keep you heart-eyes open
so you can really see

the littlest of wonders flying
into your stream,
in silent expectation,
that you may now
finally be
ready to fall in love
again
and again,

like me.

imagine

imagination is the point
where creation is given
the path, the vehicle,
and a purpose for
coming into being.

imagine all of the best things
for your you, and all,
and focus your energy
then watch, in awe,
as your world grows
more beautiful with each
divine breath you take.

imagine with all of your might
and bring into being
the goodness, the love
and the brightest light
that you wish upon
this life and this world.

imagination is not only
a thought in your mind,
it's rather the doorway to
the energies and mysteries
as yet unknown,
but completely ready
to unfold,
and to give you something
even better than gold.

create

what would you do
if your heart got to choose?
what would you make,
and birth into this world?
what would you draw up,
and what would you build?

transmuting the energy
from a thought to a thing
is actually more glorious
than we could believe.

thinking back on it,
something seemingly so simple
is powered by the
laws of the universe
and its mysterious ways.

isn't it wonderful,
how capable we can be
when we choose
and when we put
our energy
to good use?

only do the things
you can be proud of
deep inside
create
first from your heart
and
then from your mind.

high frequencies

frequency is an
energy vibration
with the potential
of full elevation

think of it as a fan
solid when static
and anti-climactic
but invisible when it's
spinning circles so dramatic

lower frequencies are
more solid to the eye
while high frequencies
might human vision defy.

as we move into

higher frequencies each

and everyone will reach

a new potential

to learn and teach.

higher frequencies

are coming in

to raise our minds

and hearts

to our potential

coded and encoded and

hidden

within.

gratitude

a most important filter
reflecting the colours of our ways
is the essence of gratitude
that we must carefully sew
within the mandalas of our days.

being thankful every moment
for everything we have and hold
focuses our energy
to that which we love.

be thankful for what you get
to taste and what you get to feel
be thankful for your shelter
and all that is true and real.

don't forget to also thank
the surprise reflections of the day,

the signs

the comforts

and the love

the universe sends your way.

make a point to do it daily

show your gratitude and care,

for those you love the most

on this journey that you share.

allow

creation and energy
must move through you
in order to become,
you must allow it to
and you must allow it through

allow your wishes to come
into the world that is
all yours

allow your dreams to become
something that you can feel
and more than just think of

allow your thoughts to flow
your laughter to roll
and your tears too

allow everything
you have always kept inside
to swing in and out
of your being

allow what you like,
and what you don't
to follow that very path
that your soul once chose.

opportunities

the world is opening up
to allow you to be you
what are you going to build?
what are you going to do?

you can make it happen
go make your dreams come true
whatever they may be
allow them to come through

be the way you want
and dream your whole way
through
a new life beginning
a new way of being

oana stefanescu

opportunities are opening

up in every way

for you.

purpose

we came into this life
with a purpose
that we immediately forgot

as soon as we stepped
out of mother's womb
the cold made us forget

all the planning
and all the zeal
of all we will do
when we come

how we will grow our souls
how we will change the world
how we will break the mold

of the structures
and the thoughts
that are holding

back
the evolution
and expansion

so close to breaking though
yet, we forgot
the true power
of our thoughts
and our energy
in body form

then again,
we had to forget
in order to
remember
that we are here
with a purpose
prewritten in our hearts

it's about time

to start reading

and feeling

what our path

is asking us to do.

impact

the power of your thought
is deceiving
seeming to be simple

the power of your thought
is permeating
more than you imagine

the power of your thought
can move
and shape your universe

the power of your thought
can change
your present and future

the power of your thought
can shift
the reality you're living

the power of your thought

is something

to direct with intention

the power of your thought

is everything

you need for impact.

discover

it is time to discover
who we really are
behind our soft skin
our bruised hearts,
and our smiling eyes.

our shell, an organic vessel,
allows us to be in this
dynamic experience
that feels so real,
but there is
more to this story.

can you feel it?
can you feel the mysteries,
as they rise higher to the surface
of the earth,
and of ourselves,
to meet us?

we are just getting started,
here in this experience,
just starting to get to know
why we are here.

we are not here to change the world,
we are here to change ourselves
only then can the world evolve
into the magnificence
she was destined for.

it is time to discover
who we really are,
what we truly desire,
and what we are capable of.

as the star-keepers that we are,
let us uncover more.

the stars within us

my heart is full, now
that you have taken
this walk with me,
and listened to these words

that so purposefully moved
right through me
and made their way to you.

these thoughts and words,
they come to me complete
in a decisive tone,
because that voice is ours

and our collective voice
wants us to hear,
to listen
and to remember that

we have the stars within us.

the kind that our eyes can see
and bigger still
all that we can only dream of,
we are all that
and so much more.

we are magnificent beings,
movements of light
expressions of energy
with so much potential
unexplored, explosive,

loving and dreaming potential
that has created universes,
including the very one
which, at the moment,
we call life.

everything is energy
and everything is entwined,

as we are part of everything
and everything is part of us.

the light and the dark
are polarities
that work together
so hard
to shape us into love.

we are all family
glorious, potent, undiscovered
yet once we do,
we will transform,
and this world too,
into happiness we haven't known
but that is waiting, ready
to ignite our hearts
and our inner
divine lights.

if you remember just one thing

from everything,

remember that you are

your own key

you are the power

of the universe itself

and when you feel called,

whisper to yourself,

I am

you are

we are

the stars within us.

thank you

Dear reader,

Thank you so much for joining me on this profound journey of spiritual discovery. I hope that our walk together has brought you joy, empowerment, and inspiration.

If you enjoyed my work and found it meaningful, please share this book with a like-minded friend. If you also have the chance of writing an amazon review for *the stars within us – high frequency spiritual poetry*, that would mean a lot to me.

I appreciate your presence here with me, along with the words, thoughts, and the energy we shared.

All the blessings to you,

Oana

acknowledgements

Before I sign off on my very first poetry collection, which has waited for many years in my heart before finally deciding to emerge into the world, I would like to offer a few words of gratitude.

First, I would like to thank my parents. Thank you for supporting and encouraging my artistic creativity and endeavours my whole life, and for crossing worlds to be able to offer me the opportunities that I have today.

To Alex, my husband and soulmate, thank you for all of the positive encouragement, support, guidance, and comfort over the years. You have always been there to cheer me on with everything I always wanted to do, including this very book. Thank you for helping me make it possible, you are the best!

Thank you to my brother, David, for guiding me with my book cover concept. Thank you also for being a constant creative inspiration, a strong supporter of my projects, and always a voice of cheerful and warm encouragement.

I also want to add a thank you to my babies, my Daniel and Leo, who fill my heart with so much love and happiness that words can barely describe, and for whom I am always learning and striving to be the best that I can be. Publishing a book has been my biggest dream, and I wanted to accomplish it in the hopes that it'll inspire you to capture your own dreams when you are ready.

In love and gratitude,

Oana

about the author

Oana Stefanescu is a school teacher, a writer, a visual artist, a mom, and the author of *the stars within us – high frequency spiritual poetry*.

Gifted with strong psychic abilities and a deep connection with the unseen realm since childhood, Oana felt a natural calling to become an energy healer and a teacher. She has developed her own energy healing modality which she applies intuitively and with purpose in healing sessions, and infuses into everything she creates, including her writing and her art.

Oana has university degrees in English Literature, in Art History and Theory, and in Education. She is also a certified Reiki Master.

Born in Romania, Oana currently lives in Canada with her family.

Oana Stefanescu / Photo by Alex Stefanescu

www.ingramcontent.com/pod-product-compliance
Lightning Source LLC
Chambersburg PA
CBHW051654040426
42446CB00009B/1129